STEP INTO SCIENCE

SEEING IS NOT BELIEVING!

The Science of Shadow and Light

BARBARA TAYLOR

Random House 🏠 New York

SHADOWS AND REFLECTIONS

In this book, you can discover how and why shadows form, and you can take a closer look at the reflections in mirrors and other shiny materials.

The book is divided into five different subjects. Watch for the big headings with a circle at each end—like the one at the top of this page. These headings tell you where a new subject starts.

Pages
4–11

Light and Shadows

Transparent, translucent, and opaque materials; how light travels; shadow shapes; shadow games.

LIGHT AND SHADOWS

Make a collection of objects like the ones along the edges of these two pages. In a dark room, shine a flashlight onto each object. Which objects let the light through? Which objects keep out the light?

Some things let light go straight through them. You can see clearly through these things. They are said to be transparent. Clear glass and clean water are transparent.

Some things let light through but they scatter the light. If you look through these materials, everything looks blurred. These materials are said to be translucent. Frosted glass and tracing paper are translucent.

Many things do not let any light pass through them. You cannot see through these things. They are said to be opaque. Your body is opaque; so is this book.

In this picture can you find a transparent material, a translucent material, and an opaque material?

Going Straight

When light hits an opaque object, a dark area forms behind the object. This is called a shadow. Why doesn't light bend around objects and light up the shadow area? To find out, try this test.

1. Cut two pieces of cardboard about 8 inches square.*
2. To find the middle of the cardboard, draw a line from each corner to the opposite corner. The point where the lines cross is the middle of the cardboard.
3. Cut a hole in the middle of each piece of cardboard.*
4. Use modeling clay to fix the

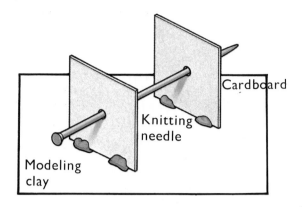

Modeling clay

Knitting needle

Cardboard

Beam of light

Make a Pinhole Camera

To investigate how light travels, try making a pinhole camera.

You will need:
An empty box, thick brown paper, tracing paper, a pin, scissors, cellophane tape, black paint, charcoal or a thick black felt pen, a dark cloth or towel.

1. Cut both ends off the box.*
2. Paint or color the inside of the box black.
3. Tape a piece of tracing paper over one end of the box.

Tracing paper

Brown paper

* *Ask an adult to help you.*

cards upright about 12 inches apart. To line up the holes in a straight line, push a knitting needle through both holes.*

5. Ask a friend to shine a light on-to the first hole. You should see the light go through the second hole.

6. Now move the second card to one side so the holes are not in a straight line. What happens?

What happens
Light travels in straight lines and cannot bend around things. So when you move the second card out of line, the light cannot get through the second hole.

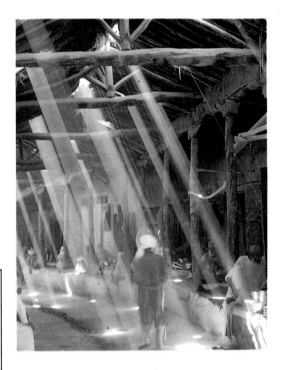

▲ Can you see the straight edges of these beams of sunlight?

4. Tape a piece of brown paper over the other end.

5. Use the pin to make a small, round hole in the middle of the brown paper.

6. Cover your head and the tracing paper end of the box with the cloth or towel.

7. Point the camera at a window and look at the tracing paper from about 6 inches away. You should see an upside-down window.

What happens
Light from the top of the window passes in a straight line through

Light from bottom of window

Light from top of window

the pinhole to the bottom of the tracing paper. Light from the bottom of the window travels to the top of the tracing paper. So the picture you see is upside down.

Shadow Shapes

Find lots of small objects and see how many different shadow shapes you can make.

A shadow is the same shape as the outside edge of an object. To change the shape of a shadow, move the object around or move the position of the light.

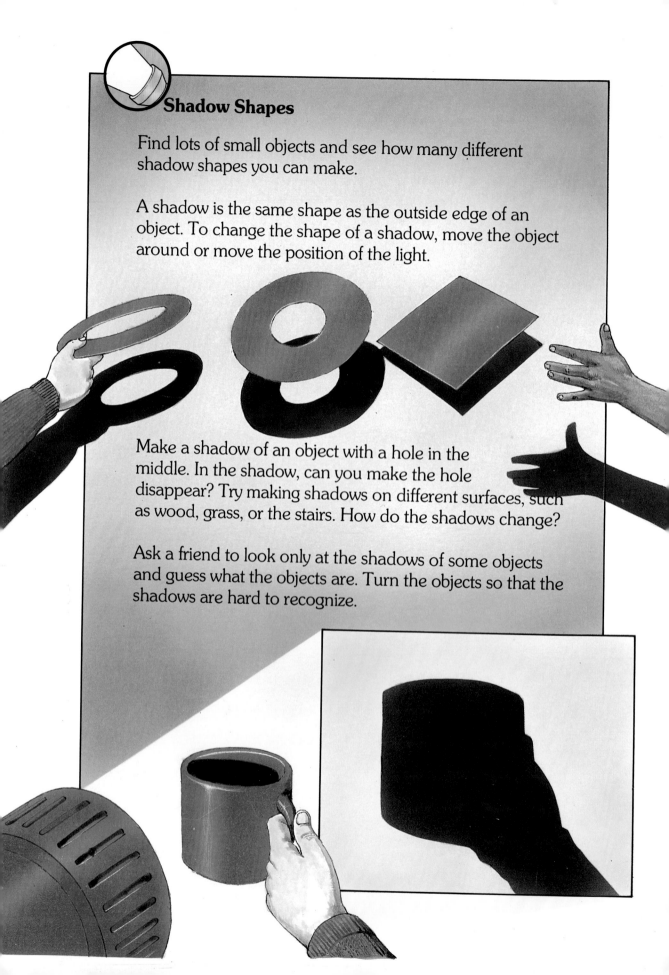

Make a shadow of an object with a hole in the middle. In the shadow, can you make the hole disappear? Try making shadows on different surfaces, such as wood, grass, or the stairs. How do the shadows change?

Ask a friend to look only at the shadows of some objects and guess what the objects are. Turn the objects so that the shadows are hard to recognize.

Shadow Portraits

1. Ask a friend to sit sideways on a chair near a wall.
2. Use masking tape to fix a sheet of paper to the wall behind your friend's head.
3. Shine a flashlight so your friend's head casts a shadow on the paper.
4. Draw around the edge of the shadow with the pencil.
5. Paint inside the outline.

Animal Shadows

You can make animal shadows with your hands. Here are some ideas. How many more can you discover?

Shadow Games

Can you hide your shadow?
Can you escape from your
shadow?

Can you shake hands with a
friend's shadow if your hands are
not touching?

Hide your shadow

Escape from your shadow

Shake hands

Can you catch your friend's shadow? If he is standing on the shadow of a tree or a building, then he is safe and cannot be caught. If you put a foot on his shadow, it's his turn to try and catch your shadow.

Can you make your shadow touch the top of the tree?
Or reach into places where you cannot go?

Shadow catch game

Long shadows

Can you fit inside your friend's shadow?

Can you jump on your friend's shadow?

Jump on a friend's shadow

BIG AND SMALL SHADOWS

With an adult's help, cut out a star shape from a piece of cardboard and fix it to a pencil with modeling clay. Prop up a large piece of white paper on some books. In a dark room, shine a flashlight onto your star so its shadow falls on the white paper.

Hold the star near the flashlight.

How big is the shadow?

Now move the star farther away from the flashlight.

What happens to the shadow? Is it bigger or smaller?

What happens to the size of the shadow if you keep the star in one place and move the flashlight backward and forward?

What happens

When the star is near the light, it blocks out a lot of light, so the shadow is big. When the star is farther away from the light, it blocks out less light, so the shadow is smaller.

Long and Short Shadows

On a sunny day, find a safe area of concrete or asphalt—not out in the street. Ask if you can use chalk to draw around shadows. With a friend, stand in the same place in the early morning, at midday, and in late afternoon. Take turns standing still while one of you draws around the other's shadow.

Measure your shadows from head to toe. How does the size of the shadows change at different times of the day? In which direction do your shadows point at different times of the day—north, south, east, or west?

Compare your shadows on a summer's day with your shadows on a day in winter. How are they different?

What happens
In the early morning or late afternoon, the sun is low in the sky and shadows are long. At midday, the sun is high above you and your shadows are shorter. In winter, the sun is lower in the sky than it is in summer. So winter shadows are longer than summer shadows.

You will need: a pencil or a short stick, an empty thread spool, glue or modeling clay, a large piece of white paper.

Make a Shadow Clock

You can use shadows to help you tell the time. Here's how to make a shadow clock.

1. Stand the pencil or a short stick in the thread spool.
2. Use glue or modeling clay to fix the spool to the piece of white paper.
3. On a sunny day, put your shadow clock outdoors where the sun will shine on it.
4. Draw a line along the shadow of the stick and write the time at the end of the line.
5. Do the same thing every 15 minutes.

½ past 11

¼ past 11

11 o'clock

¼ to 11

½ past 10

¼ past 10

10 o'clock

◀ A sundial is a type of shadow clock which was invented more than 3,000 years ago, long before watches were made.

15

Shadows in Space

The moon has no light of its own. It shines because it reflects light from the sun. Sometimes, the Earth moves in a direct line between the moon and the sun and stops sunlight from reaching the moon. The Earth's shadow makes the moon look very dark for a while. This is called a lunar eclipse. "Lunar" means having to do with the moon.

Try this investigation to see how a lunar eclipse works.

Use a large beachball or a soccer ball as the Earth and a Ping-Pong ball or other small ball as the moon. Stick a piece of string to the "moon" so you can hang it in front of the "Earth." Use a flashlight or a table lamp as the sun.

Shadow

Small ball

Large ball

Can you make the "Earth" cast a shadow on the "moon"? What happens to the shadow if you move the "moon" in a circle around the "Earth"?

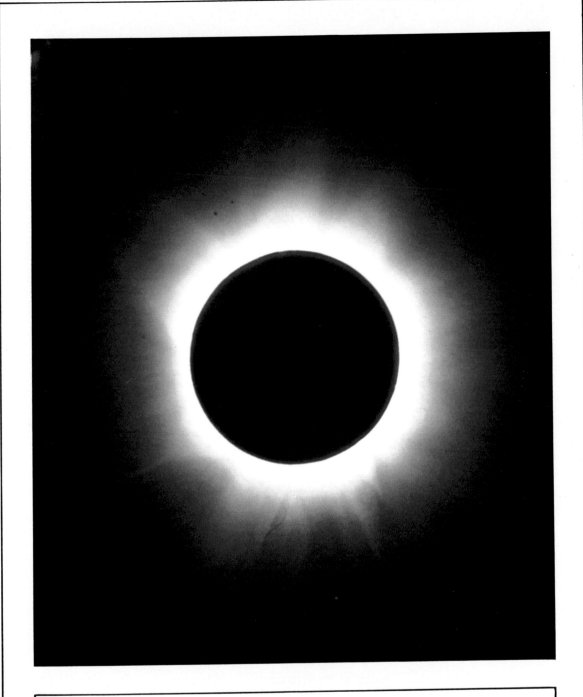

▲ This photograph shows what happens when the moon passes in front of the sun. It stops sunlight from reaching the Earth and makes some places on Earth dark during the daytime. This is called a solar eclipse—"solar" means having to do with the sun.

For a solar eclipse to happen, the moon, the sun, and the Earth all have to be in a straight line. This does not happen very often.

Reflections and Materials

How many things can you find in which you can *see* your reflection? Look for your reflection outdoors in store windows, car hoods, and buildings. Can you *see* your reflection in water? What happens to your reflection if the water is moving?

In a dark room, shine a flashlight onto different materials such as aluminum foil, brick, wood, plastic, cloth, and metal. Which materials give the best reflections?

Compare a smooth piece of foil with a wrinkled piece of foil. Can you *see* your face in both pieces of foil?

Make a collection of shiny materials. You could sort your collection into groups according to the materials the objects are made of—metal or nonmetal, for example.

Mirror, Mirror

Smooth, shiny surfaces produce the best reflections. This is why mirrors are made of a flat sheet of glass with a thin layer of shiny metal, such as silver or aluminum, behind the glass.

To make your own mirror, glue a piece of aluminum foil to a piece of thin cardboard. Make sure the foil is smooth and has no wrinkles. What can you see in your mirror? Is it as good as a real mirror? How are the reflections different?

How many different mirrors can you find at home, at school, along the street, or in a store? What shapes and sizes are they? How are they used?

▶ Dancers and actors would find it difficult to put on their makeup without a mirror.

Look in the Mirror

Look at your reflection in a mirror. Does your reflection do what you do?
Touch your right ear. Which ear does your reflection touch?

Your reflection seems to be touching its left ear. The reflection is the wrong way around and does not show you as other people see you.

A reflection does not come from the surface of a mirror. It seems to be behind the mirror. Try measuring the distance between you and the mirror. You will find that your reflection appears to be the same distance behind the mirror as you are in front of it.

Mirror Maze

To find out more about the reflections in mirrors, play this game with your friends.

1. Draw a large star shape on a piece of paper.
2. Draw a second star just outside the first one.
3. Use some books to prop a large mirror upright on a table. Or ask a friend to hold the mirror for you.
4. Hold a large book in front of your star maze so you can see the reflection but not the actual drawing.
5. Now, looking only in the mirror, try to draw around the maze without touching either of the lines.
6. How fast can you do this? Can your friend beat your fastest time? If she touches the lines, she must start again.

First star

Second star

Mirror Writing

Write your name in big letters on a piece of paper. Hold the paper in front of a mirror. Can you read your name? What has happened to the letters?

Many ambulances have the word "AMBULANCE" written back to front on the outside of the vehicle. This is so that other drivers see the word the right way around when they look in their rearview mirrors. It helps drivers to spot an ambulance coming up behind them.

Hold up this book behind your head and look at the picture below in a mirror. In your mirror, is the word the right way around?

Secret Mirror Code

You can use a mirror to invent your own secret code. Only someone with a mirror will be able to read your messages.

The trick is to write your messages while looking only in the mirror. Write each letter slowly so it looks correct in the mirror. Don't look down at the piece of paper.

When you have finished your message, it will look strange because the letters are upside down. Some of the letters will not change. Which ones are they?

25

Matching Quiz

Some things can be divided by an imaginary line into two parts that look exactly the same. These things are called symmetrical objects. You can find out if something is symmetrical by putting a mirror along the dividing line. If the object looks the same in the mirror, it has a kind of symmetry.

See if you can guess which of the objects below are symmetrical. Test them by holding a mirror against each picture.

Leaf

Orange

Scissors

Snowflake

Shell

Flashlight

Glove

Tennis racket

Cup

Feather

Key

Spoon

Funny Faces

Is your face symmetrical? Find a photograph of yourself which shows your whole face from the front. Hold a mirror down the middle of the photograph. Look at both sides of your face. Does your face look strange?

 Mirror Painting

To make a symmetrical painting, you will need: newspaper, plain paper, poster paints, jar of water, paintbrush, apron.

1. Put on the apron and lay some newspaper on a table or on the floor so you won't make a mess.
2. Mix several different colors with the poster paints. Make each color fairly thick.
3. Use the brush to drop or brush paint onto one side of the paper.
4. Fold the paper over and press down to smooth out the paint.

What happens

When you open the paper, you will have a painting that is the same on both sides, just as if you were looking in a mirror.

Reflections are caused by light bouncing off things. When this light is reflected into our eyes, we are able to see things.

Catch the Light

Use a small mirror to reflect a spot of light from the sun or a lamp onto a wall. If you turn the mirror a little, the light spot will move too. Ask a friend to make another light spot on the same wall. Can your friend touch your light spot with the one he has made?

Bouncing Back

When light hits a smooth surface, it always bounces back at a matching angle. To see how this works, try this test.

You will need: a large mirror, two cardboard tubes, a flashlight, some books.

1. Use the books to prop the mirror upright.
2. Hold one tube at an angle with the end touching the mirror.
3. Ask a friend to hold the second tube at a matching angle.
4. Shine the flashlight into the tube you are holding.

Flashlight   Tube   Mirror   Tube   Reflected light

What happens

When the tubes are at the correct angle, the light will bounce off the mirror and down to the end of the second tube. If your friend holds her hand at the end of the tube, she will see a circle of reflected light.

On a rough surface, light is not reflected like this. It is scattered back in several different directions.

29

▲ These rows of mirrors reflect the sun's rays onto the tower, which is a solar heat collector. This concentrates a lot of the sun's energy in one place. The mirrors turn to follow the path of the sun as it moves across the sky. Solar power is used to generate electricity, to heat and cool buildings, and to power small objects such as watches and calculators. Using energy from the sun does not use up any of the Earth's resources or cause pollution.

See-through Brick

Can you make a light go through a brick?

You will need: a brick, a flashlight, a piece of cardboard, 4 small mirrors, modeling clay, scissors.

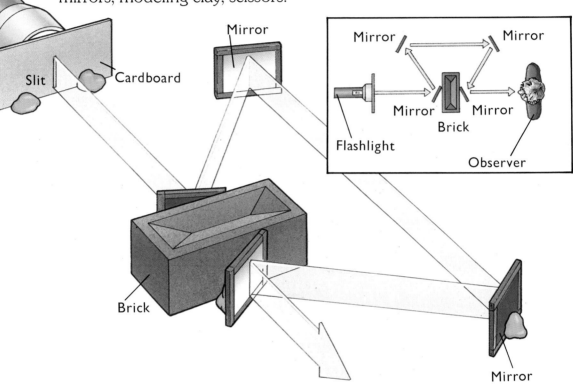

1. With an adult's help, cut a narrow slit about 2 inches deep in the middle of the piece of cardboard.
2. Use some modeling clay to prop the cardboard upright.
3. Place the brick a little way in front of the card.
4. Use the modeling clay to fix the mirrors to match those in the picture.
5. Shine the flashlight through the slit.

What happens

The light bounces from one mirror to another and looks as if it is coming straight through the brick.

Multiplying Mirrors

When two mirrors are held together at an angle, the light bounces back and forth between the mirrors. This means you can see more than one reflection of an object.

Tape two mirrors together along one of the long sides. Use some modeling clay to stand the mirrors upright at a wide angle. Put a small object in front of the mirrors. How many reflections can you see?

Now move the mirrors closer together. Count how many reflections of the object you can see now.

Your Other Face

You can use two mirrors to see yourself as other people see you. To see how this works, you need to make one side of your face look different from the other side. You could use face paints to do this.

Look in one mirror and remember where the painted side of your face appears on your reflection. Then hold two mirrors facing each other at an angle. Move the mirrors until you can see your whole face at the point where the two mirrors join. The painted side of your face will now be on the other side of your reflection.

What happens

With the mirrors at an angle, the reflection of the left side of your face bounces across to the right-hand mirror. And the reflection of the right side of your face bounces across to the left-hand mirror. When other people look straight at you, they see your face this way around.

How Many Reflections?

Hold a small mirror facing a large mirror so the small mirror is just in front of your nose. As you look over the top of the small mirror, you will be able to see lots and lots of reflections stretching away into the distance. How many reflections can you see? Are all the reflections the same size?

Make a Periscope

Have you ever had your view blocked by a crowd of people? By making a periscope you will be able to see over their heads so you won't miss anything. You can also use a periscope to look around a corner or over a wall without being seen.

Hole

Hole

Mirrors

You will need: a large empty milk or juice carton, two small mirrors, cellophane tape.

1. On one side of the carton, cut three of the edges to make a lid you can lift up. (Ask an adult to help you.)
2. Cut two holes in opposite sides of the carton, to match the picture.
3. Tape the two mirrors inside the carton. The mirrors should be facing each other at the same angle.
4. Tape down the lid.
5. Hold the periscope upright and look into the bottom mirror.

What happens

The light bounces from one mirror to the other so you can see over people's heads or around corners.

34

Using periscopes, even people at the back of a large crowd can see what is happening at the front.

Make a Kaleidoscope

The word "kaleidoscope" means "beautiful to look at." If you make a kaleidoscope, you will be able to see lots of beautiful symmetrical patterns.

You will need: stiff cardboard, a pencil, scissors, black paper or a thick black felt pen, aluminum foil, glue, clear plastic, tracing paper, cellophane tape, small colored shapes or beads.

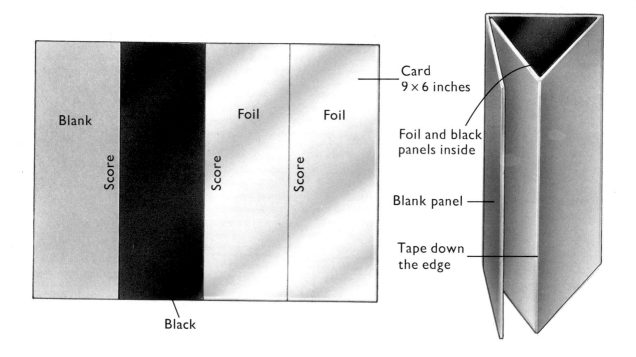

Blank

Score

Black

Score

Foil

Score

Foil

Card 9 × 6 inches

Foil and black panels inside

Blank panel

Tape down the edge

1. With an adult's help, cut out a piece of cardboard about 9 inches by 6 inches.

2. With the pencil, divide the card into four equal strips. Each strip should be $1\frac{1}{2}$ inches wide.

3. Ask an adult to help you score the lines so the cardboard is easier to fold.

4. Stick foil over two of the panels. Make sure it is as smooth as possible.

5. Stick black paper over the third panel or color it black.

6. Leave the fourth panel blank.

7. Fold the cardboard to make a triangular shape and tape the side to hold it in place.

Clear plastic

Tracing paper

Colored bits

Tape
down
the edge

Clear plastic

8. Stick a piece of clear plastic over each end of your kaleidoscope.

9. Put the colored shapes or beads over one piece of plastic and stick some tracing paper over the top. Leave enough room for the shapes to slide about.

10. Hold your kaleidoscope over a bright light.

What happens

The light bounces back and forth between the foil mirrors. The reflections of the colored shapes or beads make interesting patterns. To change the pattern, shake your kaleidoscope so the shapes or beads move into new positions.

CURVED MIRRORS

Curved mirrors change the size and shape of things reflected in them. Look at your reflection in the curved side of a shiny can or a pot. What do you look like?

Now try a spoon. The back of a spoon curves outward. This sort of curved mirror makes you look smaller.

What happens to your reflection in the front of a spoon?

▶ The surfaces of these curved mirrors curve both inward and outward. Look what they do to these reflections!

INDEX

Page numbers in *italics* refer to illustrations or where illustrations and text occur on the same page.

Adviser: Robert Pressling
Designer: Ben White
Editors: Nicola Barber and Annabel Warburg
Picture Research: Elaine Willis

The publishers wish to thank the following artists for contributing to this book:
Peter Bull: page headings; Peter Dennis (Linda Rogers Associates): pp. 22–27, 33; Kuo Kang Chen: pp. 4–5, 12–13, 18–19, 28–29, 36–37; John Scorey: pp. 6–11, 14–17, 20, 30–31, 32, 34, 38.

The publishers also wish to thank the following for providing photographs for this book:
35 D.G. Hodge; 7, 18, 21 Hutchison Library; 39 Spectrum; 5, 14, 30 ZEFA.

First Random House edition, 1991

Copyright © 1990 by Grisewood & Dempsey. All rights reserved under International and Pan-American Copyright Conventions. Published in the United States by Random House, Inc., New York. Originally published in Great Britain by Kingfisher Books, a Grisewood & Dempsey Company, in 1990. First published in the United States by Warwick Press in 1990.

Library of Congress Cataloging-in-Publication Data
Taylor, Barbara, 1954–
    Seeing is *not* believing!: the science of shadow & light / by Barbara Taylor.
        p.   cm.—(Step into science)
    Includes index.
    Summary: Simple experiments introduce the science of light.
    ISBN 0-679-80814-0
    1. Light—Experiments—Juvenile literature. 2. Shades and shadows—Experiments—Juvenile literature. 3. Reflection (Optics)—Experiments—Juvenile literature. [1. Light—Experiments. 2. Experiments.] I. Title. II. Series: Taylor, Barbara, 1954– Step into science.
QC360.T383   1991
535'.078—dc20   90-42974 CIP AC

Manufactured in Spain 10 9 8 7 6 5 4 3 2 1